A
SPOT - LIGHT
ON
Ancient Buddhist Followers

The Iconography of Buddhism

Endogenous Dance of Awareness

By Dave C.Harrisss'99, U.K.

(It is interplay between imagination and reasons or between mind and reflection.It was presented to me during my visit to Amida Trust, London)

A
SPOT - LIGHT
ON
Ancient Buddhist Followers

S.P. Taludkar

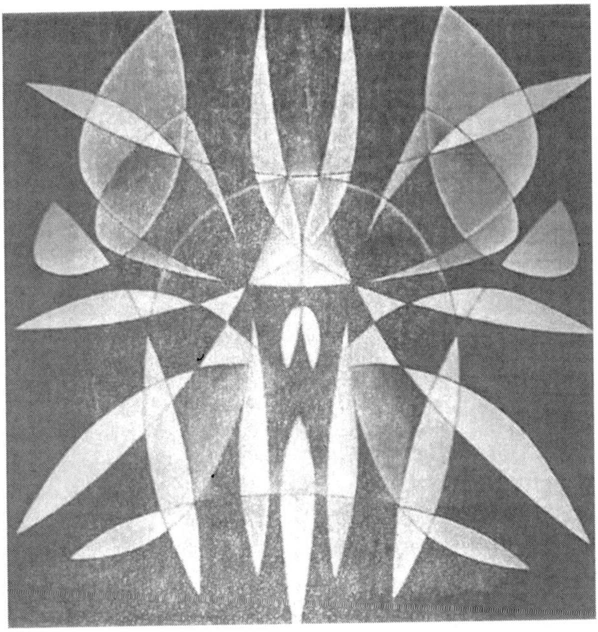

KALPAZ

ISBN : 978-93-5128-211-2

Price : ₹ 360

First Published, 2017

Published by :

Kalpaz Publications
C-30, Satyawati Nagar,
Delhi-110052
Ph. : 9212142040
E-mail: kalpaz@hotmail.com

Printed at : G. Print Process, Delhi

Cataloging in Publication Data—DK
Courtesy: D.K. Agencies (P) Ltd. <docinfo@dkagencies.com>

Taludkar, S. P., author.
A spot - light on ancient Buddhist : followers of original Buddhist doctrines / S.P. Taludkar.
pages cm
Includes bibliographical references.
ISBN 9789351282112

1. Buddhist philosophy. I. Title.

BQ4165.T35 2016 DDC 294.342 23

ON THE LAP OF SARVASTIVADIN DISTINCTIVE ELDER TENETS OF BUDDHISM.

Contents

Foreword

This is the salute to Buddhist Community. I express my gratitude to my friend T. Mag, ITS, Director, Department of Telecommunications, Govt. of India who made proof reading and gave extremely useful inputs in it.

Spot – Light to Ancient Buddhist

India is a multi-ethnic population country. One might consider the need for a census record of community basis population figure like the Buddhist Tibeto-Burman population. The census population viz :

Religion	*Number*	*Percent (Per cent)*
All Religions	1,028,610,328	100.00
Communities		
Hindu	827,578,868	85.5
Muslims	138,188,240	13.4
Christians	24,080,106	02.3
Sikhs	19,215,730	01.9
Buddhists	7,955,207	00.8
Jains	4,225,053	00.4
Religion not stated	727,588	00.1
Others	6,639,626	00.6

India as a secular country should not attach herself with religion, but most of the people are known by their religion viz Hindu majority. Gautama Buddha was born in 563 B.C. and till II CE, it was the golden era of Sarvastivada Buddhism and thereafter, it was in a state of defoliation and decadence eponymous on them. The dark ages of Buddhism occurred between 1200 and 1700 CE. In the latest census report 2001, the Buddhist Tibeto-Burman stood around 4(four) lac i.e. 0.4 per cent of the total population. They are fractionally divided into number of communities of their provenance on the basis of geographical area of living, custom, language, but they believe their ancestral origin from one. In a democratic framework of India, very little insurmountable a small community can have power to control their own affairs and also in dealing insure mountable odds. In Hinduism the supreme god is called "Brahma" with the conviction of universal unity. It is more fitting to say Tibeto-Burman are from Sakya (Shakya) race in which Gautama Buddha was born. Their origin is from the Scythian race in Central Asia. They live in the peripheries of Tibet, Burma, Bhutan, Bangladesh etc. There is likely to have a genetic link among the clans of Tibeto-Burman group of people. The evolution of theirs is still unexplored and the matter has become more complex in form with passing of time due to acculturation. Their mien indicates that they belong to Mongoloid race having 'Mongolian Fold'. They also bear the 'Mongolian Spot', a deeply pigmented patch, commonly present in the sacral region which generally disappears soon after birth'. There are close resemblances of Châkmâs with Sâkyâ race, on historical lines. Since genetic continuity exits from father to son, a DNA research project was carried out on them using the genetic variation on the Y-chromosome and other disciplinary knowledge. The study was headed by Dr Mark G. Thomas of University College, London (study No. 99/0196). What was the result remained unknown, but presumably the swab data's is now stored in the DNA Bank in USA for some particular purpose. There has also been a DNA study on genetic structure of Tibeto-Burman population of Bangladesh (Chakma, Marma, Tripura). The lower parts of the valley of the Ganges were formally occupied by people called 'Mramma' before the advent of the Aryans, eventually the gene flow occurred along the side of Bay of Bengal. There are population based studies to monopolise the country of the race with geological placement. The formation of a country is changing into a deeply ingrained oneness devoutly (religiously) It is inextricable and there is no escaping of the fact. The Buddhist Tibeto-Burman are dispersed population in different circumstances in diverse areas and yet a Sarvastivada theravada Buddhist community where they uphold faith in archaic word "Sthavir" (in profound mediation). This book attempts to delineate inner-stillness to purity instead of a pithy writing in characterisation of ancient Buddhist of Tibeto-Burman race, professing Sthavir cult of Theravada Buddhism. Arahat, Arahant and Bhikkhus, who have surpassed the egoistical state, wear saffron or maroon monastic dress of Gautama Buddha's time (Chibar) and follow traditional Buddhist rituals in Tripitaka very strictly.

Introduction

As Abraham Lincoln eloquently put it : "*If by the mere force of members of a majority should deprive a minority of any clearly written constitutional rights, it might in a moral point of view justify revolution*". In 6th century BC, the unbalanced social power and the injustices of the Vedic caste system in India prompted the development of new intellectual teaching and philosophy called "Buddhism". Shakya Muni Gautama Buddha, the founder of Buddhism (563 BC) comes down from a race or community, in modern India they are classified under the heading of indigenous Tibeto-Burman tribe. Gautama Buddha's father Suddhadhana was the ruler of Kapilavastu, the Shakya Kingdom in Nepal with neighbours as Kosala and Magadha (now in Bihar). So the term "Shakya" has aristocratic origin whose ancestry descended from Tibet (a part of Central Asia in Northern Quadrant). The term "Tibeto-Burman" has a forgone history of a mixed wave of people (India, Burma, Tibet and China) with common ancestry of Shakya line. In the ancient time, India was wealthy egalitarian society. There was nothing lacking in those days, but today India lacks in inwardly and outwardly in world's achievements. Constituent part of Shakya race continued with ancestry of 'Chakma' origin. In the 9th and 10th century AD, while Buddhism was in turmoil in Bihar, it reached Chittagong Hill Tracts from Magadh. The Chakmas number 312,000 in Bangladesh and 176,000 in India. According to legendrical history, the origin of this race held from the marriage between brother and half-sister (cousin sister) for the purity of the race, which is considered to be their major characteristics of common ancestry – now the tinniest community. There is no scientific study or documented historical or humanities study materials excepting some floating remarks that back on this subject. Basically their problem is being the result of genetic inheritance versus contact.

From 9th century onwards, Buddhism was on the decline and in 11th century AD, Turki Muslim invaded India and Buddhism was obliterated, while it reached in vertex stage during Ashoka's reign. Although the human achievements have been very vast, but yet, human knowledge does not know what is absolute or real. We can see only shadows of truth (like living in a cave) where we perceive falsely. Allegorically we see through mind and senses like a mechanism. We don't have real and true perception of life. The state of perception varies from individual to individual. For example, the perception of Socrates (c 470-399 BC), the Greek philosopher who was put to death for his advocacy that the Planet turns round the Sun (at a fixed position). This is beyond human experience and knowledge. What actually turned out to others was a heretic belief.

Another person such as Taoism (c 500 BC) Chinese philosopher advocated the concept of "Yin', the female force associated with heaven and the moon. "Yin' is complemented by 'Yang', the male force associated with the Earth and the Sun.

In the world's inflight of spirituality, there is no absolute, there is no perfect or permanent or supreme knowledge as the Universe is in rotation. There is no wiser person, but with compersion. The Universe is a complex unit, the very same with human life, by food that builds the brain as the will power or just as the will to eat develops the digestive track. It indeed leads two sides of one process and reality. One side is the excitement and the other is complete peace in sacrosanct principle.

The Chakmas are the indigenous group of people of Tibeto-Burman race, an ancient Buddhist population in the Indian sub-continent, who are known to be the last remnants of Buddhist sectorial conventions and not much with Hindu's in India. Their unswerving faith flows towards the Dhamma, the doctrine of Gautama Buddha. Their understanding differs in self liberations. Their spiritual life coasts through 'Sarvastivadin' tenets of Buddhist doctrine in Theravada Buddhism. When body and mind become one dwelling in the present moment of calm and peace,that is 'Sthavir'. That is what meditation is all about, you have to go beyond mind that put over on you (trick), tries to drive you crazy, prey on, but settles of its own accord – not because you have to do something. Without you doing, it simply settles and when stillness arises uncultivated, unpracticed, it is something superb, exquisite. If you have transformed the mind, all mind problems are solved. Not that you have found a solution, but simply they have fallen by themselves by just witnessing.

Regarding the decision of exchanging Chittagong Hill Tracts (CHT), the land of 98% Buddhist with Ferozepur (Muslim dominated land) contravened the basic partition policy of dividing the British colonial Indian sub-continent for homeland of the Hindu and the Muslim. The Buddhist had fallen between the waves of crests and the shocking announcement of the Boundary Commission for allocating CHT to Pakistan without any protest from the then Hindu leaders who otherwise believed it would be a part of India. The decision was influenced by ultimate realism of political power and strength, so prized in the hands of top Hindu leaders at that time. It shows they treated Buddhism unalloyed with Hinduism who was un-paternalistic. This remained a politically intrigued question. The Chakmas lost their home place and sheeting down lonely on the axis of two majorities in extreme embattled position. It was the improbity of top brass of both sovereign government of India and Pakistan what they were on about! The tick goes to Boundary Commission, the sole reason for this seeming inability to use good sense towards the traditional Buddhist people and denigrated them with a sense of otherness. Before this break up, the ancient Buddhist community was happy as a sandboy and from that time forth, they are in a cleft stick. Both the Hindu and the Muslims carry the world before them; but what about the Ancient Buddhist in India?

The survival of human race in the universe is eternal ('Sassata' – never ending). Despite quite of survival struggles persist every moment like the light and darkness, good and evil, creation and destruction, the natural way of human society (two forces in nature) is interminable. In Buddhism, the planet in which the living beings exist, gives an inscrutable look with curiosity to know what is inner and outer of the planet and human body through intellectual wisdom. The earliest known method of making known was "Sati Pattana Sutta", in English it is 'mindfulness', experiencing changes through breathing with 'Samata'. This was earlier known teaching of Gautama Buddha.

These ideals are the basic foundation of the Chakmas who are now scattered and running on to all directions to escape from life in a dread spectre conditions and have made good to many countries that gave them shelters. They are now like dune moved by the wind and struggling on their feet. It entails their profiling but not developed to make them of now.

The most important feature of a little nugget of Buddhist Chakmas is that they are not in their mechanism, and also not anti of any system rule. They believe in self liberation, who turned excessively small in number across the border that did not fetch up in a state. As a result, they became stateless in India. This writing is based on empirical studies and concerted passage (a crystal-glazing situation from the administrative authorities) in revelatory note of letter below:-

Shri R. Natarajan, IAS,
Deputy Commissioner,
Mizo District,
Aijal.
Dated 18th Sept. '68.

D.O. No.ACAD.16/68/19

I have been receiving your D.O. letters as well as regular reports about conditions of Chakmas in your area. I am glad that you have been devoting your full attention to the problems of Chakmas and have been trying your utmost to uplift these backward people, despite very great handicaps that you face both personally and in the discharge of your official duties due to difficulties in communication, want of security, and serious dependence on the security forces. I have taken note of all the points that you have made in your letters but I am afraid that due to difficulties in obtaining proper resources it would not be possible to accede to all the points. The SIB have recently established a WT station at Chawngte which you can use.

I would suggest that you come over to Aijal for a few days and discuss with us various matters which you may have on your mind for the improvement of your area.

(R. NATARAJAN)

Shri S.P. Talukdar,
Administrative Officer,
CHAWNGTE.

NB : It bears the testimony of primary source of events, including contemporary. The sematic history from pre – Buddhist era of Chakmas is genetic inheritance versus contact and most recent venomous.

Introspection

Man is born as a seed with potentiality (ability for development of success). However, human potential do not germinate if bereft of education which is the bridge between the potentiality and actualisation. In the mechanised world, intellectualism is based on many factors of intensiveness. There is a power to control one's own affairs within a democratic framework. Those deprived of these will be in a state of decadence. So the basic necessity is education and power to control one's own affairs. The modern world has made people more cunning, intelligent with many faces of falsehood viz – untrue heart and mind. Presently human mind is occupied in a subliminal advertisement of world progress. In Buddhism, the world is experienced through concentration of mind with own thoughts alone and action. Purification of Mind is achieved by following the precepts in "**Satipaṭṭhāna Sutta**" (Sutras in Pali). 'Prajna' is fully liberated intelligence which is explained in "**Paramita Sutta**" (Heart Sutra). The most leading monk Nagarjuna analysed it from 'Abhidhamma' in Pali.

In 300-700 C.E, some high intellectuals of Buddhism and Hinduism shared space in debate viz – Asanga, Vasubandhu, Dignaga and Dharmakriti on the Buddhist side and Vatsyana, Sabara, Vyasa, Uddyotakara and Kumarila on the other. In fact, religious doctrine of 'Vedas' was earlier to around 1500 BC and systematic philosophers grew up gradually through attempts to understand and realise more rationally. Gautama Buddha appeared in 560 B.C. After 700 C.E, things acquired a more sectarian edge as the "Astika" began to direct a fierce and unrelenting attack on Buddhist thoughts. The symbol 'Astika', 卐 representing the belief in God, is based on metaphysics (God + I). In Buddhism, 'I' is illusion, false like wave of sea coast. This symbol is refutation of Buddhist idea about the power to control, the management of the Buddhist people within the democratic framework i.e. with a representative of the government. In Buddhism, there is nothing to hold you down, everything is to be understood impermanent to be empty (Maha Prajna Paramita Sutta), emptiness refer to the world as void. So towards happiness, get rid of attachment and craving (tanha). Human knowledge begins in mother's womb and combines with a whole of life starting from births as follows:-

1. At 4 years, one learns, 50% of the whole knowledge
2. At 7 years, one learns, 75% of the whole knowledge
3. At 18 years, brain becomes fully developed.

Gautama Buddha attained enlightenment at the age of 35 years. After destroying the disturbances of the mind, and attaining concentration of the mind, he attained insights (Vipassana) which led to enlightenment. The Sthaviravāda, one of the early Buddhist schools from which the Theravada-tradition originates, emphasised sudden insight. They come from nowhere and go nowhere, they are not permanently established as an entity anywhere, they are perfection of forbearance.

A small number of people in the west of Nepal in Tansen area still believe to be descended from the genealogical tree of Sakya race. A small number of people who claim to be the Sakya are also living in Kargil, Gandhara beside other places in North West India. There connotations Sakyas: similar to Sak tribe in Myanmar, the earliest race who occupied the lower part of the Ganges and far distant coastal regions of the Bay of Bengal in the East. Looking at the map, we will notice the Himalayan

Mountain ranges slopes down towards the Bay of Bengal over a region, which is known by the name "Chittagong Hill Tracts" (CHT), now in Bangladesh. Prior to 600 B.C, there had been a lot of movement of people within the river valley of the Ganges of India and the Irrawady in Myanmar. Myanmar or Mramma or Brahma i.e. the 1st inhabitant of the world, is a term applied to the inhabitants of Burma by the Aryan settlers. Consequently they divide into factions – the Pyu, the Kanran and Mramma. They do not maintain their link on the footprints on their ancestors. Nevertheless, some do have an oral history that intersects and sometimes blend with the Sakya race, who have changed in space and time.

"It is probable that the lower part of the valley of the Ganges was formerly occupied by people language called 'Mramma' before the advent of the Aryans; but, as regards, the Burmese, it seems more natural to believe, as Sir. Arthur Phayre writes, that they passed from the table land of Central Asia round the Eastern Himalayas. (......). The hill tribes of Arakan who live near the Kuladan river and its tributaries, namely the Sak, Chaw, Kwaymi, Kun, Mro and Shandu, belong by origin to the same Mramma group the Burmese, and their language belongs to what is sometimes called the Tibeto-Burman family." The Arakanese, and their akin groups differ but little in feature from the Burmese; and though their spoken language is so dissimilar from that of the latter as to be almost unintelligible, but when written it is the same in all most all respect. Sâkyâ history was recorded in 'Digho-atthokatha' and 'Suttanipitaka-attahakatta'. On Sâkyâ king Abhiraja's death, his two sons divided the kingdom and the elder ruled over Arakan and the younger the Burma. During the Gautama Buddha's life time, 50,000 Sâkyâs were massacred in one day in Kapilavastu, not even sparing the women and children. This is the worst disaster as recorded in the Pali texts mentioned above. The reign of king *Vidudabha* of Kosala is darkened by the terrible atrocity, which he perpetrated on the Sakyas. Apparently he did that to avenge their treachery in marrying *Visabha Khattiya*, a slave girl, to his father. However, his real motive in invading the territories of the Sakyas could be to destroy their autonomy completely. We do not know anything more about *Vidudhaba* or his successors when the curtain raised again. Those who survived were driven out of their original land, now in Nepal and the Sakya prince *Dhaja Raja* moved into Burma and he married the widow of *Binakya Raja* of Burma (Myanmar) as they were of Sakya race. The 'Burman' is the blood brother of Buddhist Shakya race of India before the arrival of the Aryans and at some period of time the Buddhists were driven out from India. *Dhaja Raja* with his followers made his way through Kubo valley (now in Burma) before entering into the Irrawady valley and Arakan and distant mountain areas. Some of them established new kingdom in far distant Himalayan mountain ranges to the east. Their memory of their ancient past gradually faded. The term 'Burman' indicates a class of people in Hindu society and the term 'Tibeto-Burman' is applied to the people from Burman peninsula and the river basin of Brahmaputra (known 'Sangpo' in Tibet). In the chronological table of historical events, 'Sakya' were the earlier settlers on this land.

They are now discriminated, not possessing any hold over their land and thereby have become a forgotten race in the new era. They still exist, however, as tribes claiming to be of Sakya race. The Centre for Genetic Anthropology, University College, London has taken up a DNA study: a study of relationship of Y-chromosomes in the Sakyas.

The sub-regional area between Arakan and the southern Bengal was known to be Chittagong Hill Tracts, now in Bangladesh and the people inhabiting there are known to be Châkmâs. While reviewing the census of India, one British

Scholar has written, "in my belief that one of the most meaningful service that the ethnographic survey can do to trace the CHT hill Tribes: Chakmas. The semantic detailed meaning of the term Chakmas, who are these people and their provenance? How little the people of the world are aware about them? There has been no well documented record of history of native Chakmas. A tangible record from Eastern Bengal Gazetteers: Chittagong by L.S.S O. Malley, ICS is quoted here: "Such a border chieftain (practiced a sort of nomadic husbandry) was found in one Jan Baksh Khan who in 1784 greatly disturbed the peace of the hill borders (now CHT). The Collector submitted an elaborate plan from excluding him from all communications with the low country, but the Calcutta authorities recommended moderation and ordered the Collector whether the hill people might not be induced by a lenient policy to become a peaceful subjects and cultivators of the low land." In earliest British record of 1808 C.E, the first range of hills bordering on the plains to the north and east of the province of Chittagong were tributary to Honourable Company (British East India) and their villages were called 'Chooms'. (Ref : Account of the Kookies or Lunctas, Asiatic Researches (vol-7) by John Macrac, page 184, 1st published in 1808). They carried in their memory, their first king was Bijoy Giri (1118 AD). Allow me to introduce a few typical specimen of them. How life has gone forth in their memories? Their past history is rather a far remote history and no provenance. A copy out passage from "The Chakmas, an ancient Buddhist Population in the Indian Sub-Continent" by Heinz Bechert may be presented here. Many events have ever taken them and they try to trace their genetic chronology from the Sakya race in which Gautama Buddha was born. In the Chakmas, there are sub-tribe by name *Doingnak,* mostly in Myanmar, and *Tungjainya,* who are believed to have broken off parent tribe in Myanmar and moved into CHT in 1819 AD. It is believed that Chakmas have a genealogical link with Arakanese for the reasons that those Chakmas who have migrated to CHT from Arakan are known *Anakya* Chakma and those who had remained in Arakan are *Rowyangya* Chakmas. Historically, 1778 AD was the beginning of an epoch making era, as the chief of the Chakma tribe, Jan Baksh Khan declared loyalty to the British Company and the whole geographical area of CHT came under the British rule with levy of annual tribute. The Chakmas were the inhabitants of the first range of hills bordering on the plains to the North and the East of the province of Chittagong till 1864, at which time the whole jurisdiction of CHT was separated from Chittagong vide Bengal Government Act XXII of 1860.

There were self perpetuating system in the Chakma society dominated by the elite (a sense of nobility) who were connected with revenue collection system of administration that came down hereditary – a kind of feudalism not as stratification, but as a matter of fact, it was an equalitarian society. In a manner corresponding to their functionaries, the titles were granted e.g. Khan (head of a clan), Roy, Dewan, Talukdar, Khisha and Karbari. This status is still passing down through social hierarchy without any procedure. In general, most people in CHT are known by the term 'Chakma' in the British historical record and Indian Constitution. 'Chakma' is pronounced in English accent and in the native language is 'Chawngma', similar to the spelling 'Yuan Chwang' in Chinese (Hiuen Tsang in English), the Chinese traveller and scholar who visited India in 7 AD. So far no official discovery is made on the origin of the word – 'Chakma', which is very akin to 'Chawngma'. I would rather not go pronouncing judgement on a subject that I know so little about. The CHT was known to be a "Choom", now "Jhoom" land and the inhabitants were called "Choomeeas', now "Jhoomeas". The *Choom* or *Jhoom* signify shifting cultivation, a life line in the forest mountain area. In medieval era, the males were known to wear hand woven dress (Jumma dress) which have been substituted by "Dhoti" (used in Bengal), but the artistic hand woven dress of Chakma women remained as typical. The upper part covering the breast is known to be "Khadi" and the lower part from waist to the bottom is known to be "Pinon". This dress must have been filtered down from fore fathers. If you permit me, I must say, if the human race be regarded by man of science, it is to be solved by scientific method through multiple knowledge how it sustained. The circumstances of Chakma's life in CHT was outworn during 1947-72 and Chakmas are now seem moving on to all directions all over as they have lost their home land as result of construction of large hydro electric project at Kaptai on Karnaphulli river in 1960. There was displacement and break up of over 60 thousand indigenous Buddhist Chakmas from their ancestral homes. A copy out passage from Adam Curlie's (a member of planning commission of the Pakistan Government) writing is quoted. Their poverty level remained persistent over time. A lot of efforts have gone into it to mitigate their suffering but it ended in deaf air of then Pakistan Government. Chakma's ancestral history can be traced in mental eye from 16 AD, but I don't know how to put it exactly as they consist of 40 sepal divisions in Chakma on male line. Permit me to pick up one ancestral history of Range – Goza which reels as follows: In 16 AD, an unthrone king became a novitiate (Monk life, in Pali 'Moisang') in a Buddhist Monastery and became known as Moisang Raj, whose genealogical chart is as below:

Family Diagram (Peerage)

Moisang Raj (16 AD)

Sumesur | Madam Thansa

Bothangsa

RajaniBibi, Kandar Khan, Indar Khan, Sundar Khan, Nirabal Khan, Mangal Khan, Kmal Khan, Jubal khan, Subal Khan, Biral Khan

Lusi Sekhar

Halumya | Nizauya | Gulumya | Manhalya

Lochan | Range Faneshar

Seekam Khan | Nimak Khan | Ramak Khan

Mukta Ram | Manu Khan

Kala Chan, Tabal Chan, Tilak Chan, Hagar Chan

Chandi Charan

Mritunjoy, Vairab Chandra and Karna Dhan

Pran Kishor, Pran Hari, Ananda from (1st Wife)

+ Birendra, Dr Pramode Bikash Chakma from (2nd Wife)

(29.11.1909-11.10.1990)

The spoken language of Chakma is very dissimilar with Burmese and Arakanese. But when written, it is almost scripturally similar in all excepting a few. Chakma script originated from conterminous areas of Eastern Bengal and Suvarnabhumi (now Burma, Myanmar), where Sakya race came in pre-Buddhist era and dispersed both at the top of the mountain ranges (Himalayas) and the bottom of it. Difference between the spoken and the script of Chakmas is such that the former falls under the group of Eastern Indian language and the latter is South Asiatic. The letters used in writing Chakma language are pronounced viz

1. Ozha pat 2. Majja pat 3. Kea pat
4. Chu-chang-kha 5. Gu-chang-kha 6. Chang-dal-gha
7. Ten-dal-ya-gha 8. Chila-vanga-ghaetc

In 1860 CE, Bengali subject was introduced in Chakma schools and before that their home education were in traditional script or writing that insinuated a feeling of goodness. Intrinsically it is important to know the provenance of Chakma script. In the modern era, the language juxtaposed (a thing beside another) to communicate widely is prized.

The Sakya had a reputation of being fierce and warlike. They were Kshatriyas, too proud to their lineage. One of the greatest sages of peace, the Buddha descended from this tribe. He is called 'Shakyamuni', which means 'Shakya Monk'. When the Buddha taught the Four Noble Truths, he began with the First Truth that states – the life is 'dukkha', the life is suffering or stressful or unsatisfactory. But the Buddha also used the word to mean 'impermanent' and 'conditioned'. To be *conditioned* is to be dependent on or affected by something else. Buddha spoke often of the Five Skandhas, also called the Five Aggregates or the Five Heaps. The Skandhas, very roughly, might be thought of as components that come together to make an individual.

Everything that we think of as "I" is a function of the skandhas. The First Skandha: Form (*Rupa*), The Second Skandha: Sensation (*Vedana*), The Third Skandha: Perception (Samjna, or in Pali, Sanna), The Fourth Skandha: Mental Formation (Samskara, or in Pali, Sankhara), The Fifth Skandha: Consciousness (Vijnana, or in Pali, Vinnana). The Buddha wove his explanation of the skandhas into many of his teachings. The most important point he made is that *the skandhas are not "you."* They are temporary, conditioned phenomena. The Buddha taught that the skandhas were dukkha.

Commenting on his reaction on a simple Buddhist rite, Levi-Strauss wrote: "This great religion of non-knowledge is not based on our inability to understand. It bears witness to that ability and rise us to a pitch at which we can discover the truth in the form of a mutual exclusiveness of being and knowledge. Through an additional act of boldness, it reduces the metaphysical problems to one of human behaviours - a distinction it shares only with Marxism It's schism occurred on the sociological level, the fundamental difference between the Great and the Little ways being the question of whether the salvation of a single individual depends, or does not depend, on the salvation of humanity as a whole."

The universe is a complex unit, the very same with human life - by food that builds the brain, just as the will power or as will to eat develops the digestive track. Indeed, there are two sides of one process and reality – one side is the excitement and the other is complete peace on sacrosanct principle. The Sanskrit word 'Pratitya – Samutpada' in Theravada means dependent arising that phenomena (Dharma) exists in relationship to all other things, one generating the other. Buddha had often expressed his experience of Enlightenment in one of two ways, either in terms of having understood the Four Noble Truths or in terms of having understood the nature of the dependent origination. The method of 'Pratitya – Samutpada' should be understood as follows:- Because of A arises B. Because of B arises C. When there is no A, there is no B. When there is no B, there is no C. It is a discourse on the process of birth and death and not a philosophical theory about the evolution of the world. It deals with the cause of rebirth and suffering with a view to helping men to get rid of the ills of life. According to the Law of Dependent Origination, there are 12 Links which account for the continuity of existence birth after birth:

1. Ignorance (avijja);
2. Volitional activities (Sankhara)
3. Embryonic (in early stage of six months, sentient being is capable of feeling in mother's womb (vinnana);
4. Mind and Matter (individual consciousness, subject like illusion of sea coast (nama-rupa);
5. Six spheres of Sense. (eye , ear , nose , tongue , skin, mind) (salayatana)
6. Contact (phassa). As sentient grows, this contact experience is absorbed in memory.
7. Sensation (Vedana)
8. Craving (tanha);
9. Clinging/ attachment (upadana);
10. Action (Kamma)(bhava)
11. Rebirth (Jati)
12. Decay and Death (jara – marana)

Universal truth (Dharma) exists in relationship to all other things. The cosmos (universe) is not a closed and harmonious karmic unity system; it is a battleground of cross currents and conflicting antonyms and ambivalent purposes; it shows itself with pathetic obviousness as not a uni but a multi-verse. It gives every sign of contradiction and division within itself. It is important to recollect that whatever you create, you destroy and whatever you annihilate you create – one condition the other (one generating the other), just as the inhalation conditions the exhalations (a puff of breath, vapour), one is the karmic result (work) of the another i.e. relativism. All phenomena in this universe are relative, conditioned states and do not arise independently of supportive conditions. The fact that everything is nothing more than a set of relations is consistent with the modern scientific view of material world. Life is not alone, it is microcosm, a miniature representation of humankind viewed as epitome of the universe. Any complex unity is viewed in the way of microcosmic forms. They are linked together and build the human life as the product of creationism. The blood brushed run wild by the will, which we vaguely call life (mind and soul, men's personality, animate), build its own vessels by wearing on grooves in the body, close up and becomes arteries and veins. The will to know builds the brain, just as the will to grasp forms the hand, or as the will to eat develops the digestive track. Indeed there are two sides of one process and reality. The relation is best seen in emotion (mental feeling), where the feeling and the internal body changes from one complex unit 'microcosm', in Biology it is called cell and in physics 'atom'. Now, what manner of a man is he to understand himself – with outer physical body or inner spirituality? (Outer physical attributes viz wealth, cloth, dress are completely different from happiness and 'dukkha', because you do get physical things as you want, while the opposite is not true.) The whole thing is relativism to understand the idea of the knowledge or morality. The doctrine of knowledge, truth, morality etc. is relative and not absolute and it is not same always as the world is not static. Spirituality (relating to sacred things, animation) is antithetical to one section from another. It may be ambivalent, conflicting and serendipitous surprise viz. spirituality is guided by devout faith and it might appear cross conflicting to other non-believers. This is how world has been set with woe, woebegone etc. Hindus set forth 'Moksha' as the ultimate goal and the Buddhist "Nirvana' is the transcendental state of consciousness in this life itself. In a sense, Hinduism and Buddhism are analogous to the belief of:

1. Rebirth on the result of Karma – the cyclical unfolding of events governed by the law of cause and effect;
2. Liberation of Rebirth;
3. Both are androcentric (men - supreme).

In Buddhism, the term āgama is used to refer to a collection of discourses of the early Buddhist schools. The sutras, corresponding to the first four Nikayas (and parts of the fifth) of the Sutta-Pitaka of the Pali Canon are also occasionally called agamas. In this sense, āgama is widely used to denote the Buddhist scriptural traditions. Human life is made of 5 (five) basic elements – earth, air, fire, water and sky; and with non-elements – education, food, knowledge etc. It contains 5 (Five) senses i.e. eye, ear, nose, tongue, body and mind (anubhuti). Mind is part of experience by a perspicacious understanding through five senses. It is like illusion of sea coast, until sensation begets memory and memory begets ideas in mind, and unconscious state of mind is dream. They all are dependent origination (Dharma), phenomena exists in relationship to other things. The basic 5 (five) elements of the universe is divided into particles (extremely small pieces or amount such as proton, electron), some particles have mass (identified shape) and others do not. Scientists have discovered it.

Inset of Fulfillment

The concept of *yin and yang* has shaped Chinese thinking for more than 2000 years. Yin and Yang are the forces in nature that are thought to create balance figure, quintessence with each other. Yin (here in blue) is regarded as female, passive and earthy (coarse or crude), Yang in red is considered to be male, active and heavenly. Looking at this form of cultural epitome perspective, we seem to know why both Chinese philosophy Confucianism and Taoism (c 500 BC) accept Yin-Yang principle?

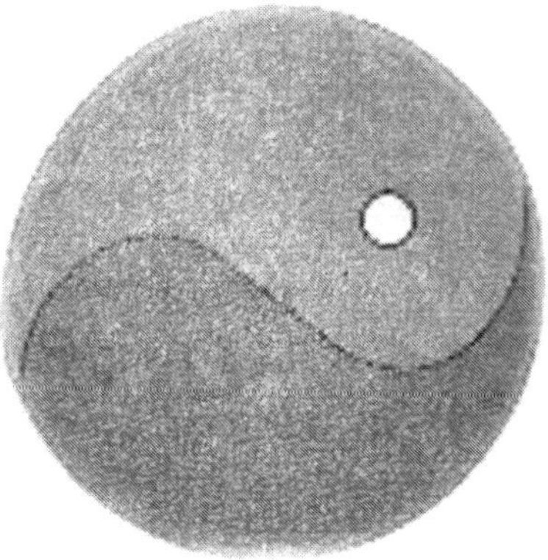

Buddhism is known as the light of Asia and the mongoloid people express the strong feeling of satisfaction. Both the Tibetan and the Châkmâ express the strong feeling of satisfaction (love) by tendering nose closer to each other orally. Châkmâs say "naak coo de" (tender the nose). Another idiomatic phrase "choong choong puhkhai" is associated with an affectionate communication with the child by hiding or covering the face with the palms and then removing the hands suddenly. Also the most loveable child is called *choong* (Dear choong). There are many terms that remained inexplicable or its root of origins. *Burpara* is social custom of Chakmas which ideologically believe in purification from all evils. They believe, one can get rid from the grief of suffering by *Burpara* on the bank of river and taking a dip into the water. These are the eastern mongoloid culture.

With the passage of time, there might have been many intrinsic traditions of acculturation among them. Those could be undefined like emptiness of original nature of our lives due to dependent arising as explained in Buddhism. There are sequel events of earlier action and sequences - one generating the other.

A NOSE RUB FOR PREZ

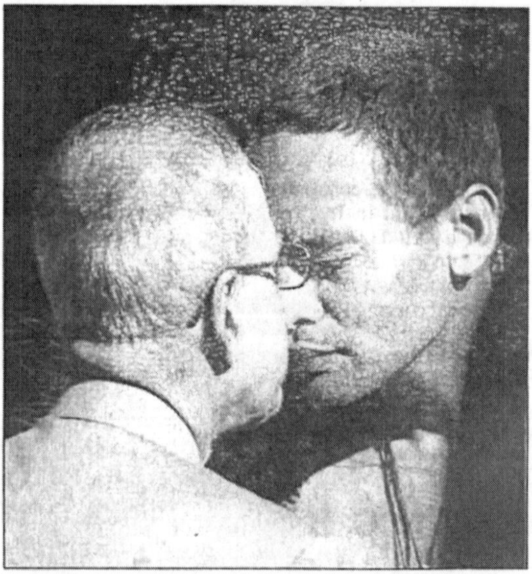

▪ President Pranab Mukherjee is welcomed with a Hongi, a traditional Maori greeting in which two people rub their noses, as he arrives in New Zealand on Saturday. AFP PHOTO

Inset of Fulfillment

The old Chakma custom *Burpara* is a symbol of emotive feeling, cleansing and purifying from all evils, spirits, curse, illness misfortune etc. from all defilements every year with crucial goal of becoming Bodhisatta, Swastika purity (卐). How has it emerged as the ideal description of life ? In Buddhism, one's central objective is to attain Nirvana, laying stress on the extinction of individuality, while that of the Hindus is to be soulfully with God. In this way of faith (religious belief), human beings are filleted into the majority and the minority groups. The Chakma people in south eastern countries of Indian subcontinent are adavist (reversion to earlier) Buddhist people, a minority who are fairly and squarely being treated with high handedness: as one says, "Yes to the stranger or by forcing the weaker to say yes to them". They are generally believed to be continuing to follow ancient traditions and their natural characteristics as reserved people (who feel impolite to tell someone that they are wrong). Consciousness comes from sight, touch, sound, smell, taste and mental objects- conscionable conscientious in the frame of mind.

Advaya – Sunnya Buddhism

Analysis

There is a philosophical term "Advaita" viz. Advaita Vedanta (Hindu) hints at conquest of all desires and sensual pleasure by practicing purity of thought, speech and action. As you go beyond self, you suddenly discover as sky that there is no limit. A few call it "God", universal unity, interconnectivity. In Vedanta, soul or yoga (derived from the Sanskrit root "**Yuj**", meaning "to join". The English word "yoke" is also derived from the same Sanskrit (Indo-European) root. Also denotes an essential part of something, noble equality) is true union with own God or link with God through "I" (ultimate truth). It assumes that the whole creation is connected for man's purpose.

In Buddhism, there is a term "Advaya" (innerstillness, sthavir purity). The literal meaning of 'Advaya' (= non dual) is "other than the two". The concept of advaya is pivotal to Buddhist thoughts. Advaya and Advaita both are from the common origin, which have almost a negligible difference in meaning, yet the former meaning 'non-dual' and the latter denoting 'monism' are conventional in Buddhist and Vedantic schools respectively which are actually diametrically opposite to each other in several contexts. Advaya in Buddhism basically negates the extreme ends. Buddha propounded the 'middle path' by condemning the extreme ends: (i) severe penance or self-mortification and (ii) licentious.

In Mahayana, in the meditation of reality, the idea is "I have never been born and I will never die". In Theravada

Buddhism's philosophy, emptiness was based solely on "analytic view of emptiness". It did not leave a total realisation of emptiness of the phenomenal things. In Prajna Paramita Sutta, it disclosed 'emptiness' as free from both being and non being. Nagarjuna's stand point of emptiness is a complete philosophical realisation. He mentioned, "Yah pratitya samutpadah sunyatam tam pracaksmahe". If anything is dependently originated, that thing does not have its own intrinsic nature (Svatantra). That is dependent always and exists when only the causes are there. The meaning of 'Sunyata' is empty of its intrinsic nature. According to the 'Prajnaparamita' literature, 'prajna' means realisation of 'sunyata'(emptiness). In order to realise that 'emptiness', one has to be devoid of view of the "Atma" (Self/ Soul). One has to have Anatta (non-self) Bhavana. This has been further elaborated in the Mogharaja Manava Puccha in Sutta Nipata.

Mogharaja Sutta (emptiness)

"Sunnato lokam avekkhassu–moghraja sada sato–attanuditthim uhacca – evam macctaru siya–evam lokam avekkhantam-maccaraja na passati". O Mogharaja, with ever mindfulness, you have to see the world (As void, having eradicated the notion of an Atma or Self). You must get rid of atta-dithi (Self view). By this way, you can cross over the Mara. If anyone sees the Loka (World) by this way, the king of the death (Maccaraja) will not see him. Here, a very important idea has been given, that is, the *Sunyata* means to get rid of self-view. In order to get rid of self-view, one has to have 'Prajna' (Wisdom). Without 'Prajna', no one will be able to realise *Anicca* (Impermanency), *Dukkha* (Suffering) and *Anatta* (non-self). In early Buddhism, the importance of 'Panna' (Prajna) is explained in the context of realisation of *Nibbana.* The Mahayana sect attempted to show it through the Prajnaparamita literature.

The sutra mentions six paramitas that the Bodhisattva has to practice: *Dana* (Generosity). *Sila* (Morality), *Ksanti* (Patience), *Virya* (Effort), *Dhyana* (Concentration) and *Prajna* (Wisdom). In Buddhism, one must earn 'Parami' (Parama + I), which means most excellent. It is marked in the sense of future Buddha, who is the most excellent one. Twenty four Buddhas appeared before Gautama Buddha and the future Buddha is known to be Moitri Buddha.

The word 'emptiness' does not mean nothingness. It means no thought, no conception, blank, no boundaries – going beyond your meditation so that your thinking can stop. As long as you have concept, there is a binding to distinction of the subject and the object, and you cannot reach at the oneness of all. So, after you free yourself from conceptual limits through Buddhist practice, you should also attain the state of 'emptiness'. That is how free Buddhism is and that is the real essence of Buddha's teaching. It gives you all the teachings, but in the end, there is nothing to hold you down. In the verse *Sagalhavagga Samyutta*, Buddha taught for the benefit of those superior persons who are capable of striving hard for complete eradication of defilements for the attainment of Arahatship in this very life. As a consequence of his strenuous efforts, if one becomes an Arahat, there is no need for him to set up a new life.

There were egoistical Sarvastivada, Mula-Sarvastivada and Mahasanghika across the time span from 4 BC to 12 AD. According to them, being Sthavira/Sunnya is the state with no more as intrinsic as before. The modern world is in diplomatic tautology (universal panacea) twisting the matter/substance over in different words keeping under the grip of the mighty with clout. Both the Theravada (Hinayana), the lesser vehicle and the Mahayana, the greater vehicle are theoretically the same. Various Buddhist traditions teach different accounts of Buddha's life.

Kalama Sutta (Solipsism = only one's own experience)

Do not believe in what you have heard; Do not believe in traditions, because they have been handed down from many generations, Do not believe in anything because it is rumored and spoken by many; Do not believe in the conjecture; Do not believe in that as truth to which you have become attached by habit: Do not believe merely on the authority of your teachers and elders; after observation and analysis when it agrees with reason and is conducive to the good and again of one and all, then accept it and live up to it.

Identified Chakma Scripts in light Of Ancient times

"Lost, it is buried ? One more missing piece ?
But nothing's lost, or else : all is translation
And every bit of lost in it" — **James Merill**

As being known in ethno-biological theories, the Chakmas are tribe of the Saka (Scythian), assuming kinship with the Burmese and the Tibetan. Historical and linguistic references are already quoted. The Chakma script is in hidden depth, which is known to be 'Ozha Path', identified with the Burmese and the Arakanese except a small variation in total. There are 38 (Thirty Eight) alphabets in the Chakma script. This emotive home dialect (language) appears to be a form of Magadhi and South-Eastern Bengali with many unexplained and unknown words.

Language maintains local relations and communications to the surrounding people. The Chakma queen Kalindi Rani used Bengali as the court language during her reign. During the colonial rule also, Bengali was the court language. Since 1870, Chakma's native language had fallen into disuse. In 1916, Dr Suniti Kumar Chatterjee (Former National professor of India) came with judgement that the "Charya Pad' is the original Bengali form, which is a Buddhist text in poetry songs. The 'Gengkhuli' songs in the Chakma language have similarities with them. The oldest Chakma literary works are Shristi Pattam, Agartara, Gengkhuli, Gozen Lama, Radhe Mohon Dhom Pudi and many others. The original writings are not traceable, which is known to have 20 set of books.

It says:

Lose your language and you lose your culture
Lose your culture and lose your identity
Lose your language and you will lose your Mutual Understandings
Lose mutual understandings and you lose Harmony, Mutual support and peace.
Lose your place you lose your brotherhood
Lose your brotherhood you will lose your identity.

Every tradition has its source in ancient rites and the Chakmas have from the Sakya race, the followers of original Buddhist doctrine. But from 1947, their identified culture reduced to menial position as they were made stateless ("One of the things everyone know but no one can quite think how to demonstrate is that a country's politics reflect the design of its culture").

Pre-dating 1947, Chakmas walked with life freely and after 1947, they walk through something and a small group of them represent conceptual change into cultural forms for power, positions, wealth, fame, the materialistic gain and the real rewards of life. In integer, are they successful? Prior to this, they were of equalitarian society.

Let me draw a light remark from childhood. Shri Shiv Charan Chakma manifested no interest in the worldly life and rather developed instinctively to spirituality and composed "Gozen Lama," the symbolic presence of Gautama. He also composed God's songs that represent the infinite God, ancient unequivocal Buddhist belief of the Chakmas. No one as yet could orchestrate it fully. The original text is untraceable but so far as the Chakma's antennary, their most attractive religious text is Gozen-Lama, the supreme creator of the Universe and the human-beings. Permit me to quote from Gozen – Lama:

In Chakma and Translation:

1. *"Jal-arupar bawiya thal; banela Gozen jib-Sakawl"*
   (On water surface, there is plainness; On it human life created by Gozen!)
2. *"Jee-Kam, Jare Sajee phal phai; Param Gozen nahidai!"*
   (Results of work, as you do (done). It related nothing to Gozen)
3. *"Hatee Lama purela Na-jebong; Ju-Ju Na-gathung Doz-gong !"*
   (Not to kill by own hand, To avoid falling in hell ages!)
4. *"Cheer Lama purele Na-jebong; Gozen – Lama bar labong"*
   (Be restive unless four lamas is complete, Get blessedness from Gozen)
5. *"Je-bar mange sei – bar – pai ; Gozen bar – dile na phurai"*
   (Whatever pray we get, Gozen's blessings expands!)

A radical change is growing to explore their folk wisdom, tales and memory in the next generation. I think, the forth-coming generations must go ahead to explore the microcosm of Buddhism (Gozen Lama) and it will bring them to themselves. Shri Pran Hari Talukdar was one time the head of range Goza of revenue circle 'Kachalong' and his sire lived in Matamohori river bordering with Arakan. He had memory of his own scripts with preciseness. There were many hermetic existence of CHT. He was self-educated with the arch of learning and knowing many ideas on many aspects of life. I find, this was his expertness and the inherited characteristics of ancestry. This has been quoted by renowned writer Shri Biraj Mohan Dewan in his book, "Chakma Jatir Itibritta." Their writing is an aspect of culture.

It is known as "UNG" in Chak[illegible] symble of a MANTRA[illegible]

The chief aim of finding identity on the basis of Language and Women's Dress

In the Indian sub-continent, the element of personal characteristic is known in the language he speaks. So it is a prerogative of the state or community to preserve languagc (India is divided into many linguistic states). From historical perspectives, the Chakmas broke in (moved) to many regions from ancient time and their script is very akin to the Arakanese and the Burmese, which might have some links with the Tamil scripts. The founder of Tamil language was Rishi Agastya who lived in Vindya mountains. It is the Tirunelveli district in Tamilnadu,King Ashoka sent his son and daughter with Parians (Tamils) to propagate the tenets of Dhamma of Gautama, Some graphical symbol of the scripts are depicted in Chakma's 'Ung', which is used in household medicament. A closer link of Pariah Tamil scripts with the Chakma script is indicated in the book *Fogiri Alan* and *Fogiri Kalam* by Sib Charan Chakma. This script is called 'Ozha Pat' (38 nos), which is now Otis. Their genetic language has been interfused with many different dialects. They realise the significance to sieve their genetic script and dialect which layered and got into : What are thc similarities and differences are with respect to Indo-Aryan and Tibeto-Burman grammatically, phonetically and otherwise. Takc for example, the Chinese philosopher Yuan Chwang in English is pronounced as Hiuen Tsang. So, one has to judge the historical and cultural and administrative reasons. The Chakmas adopted Bengali language in lieu of their genetic script and language in educational institutions since 1860. Bengali subject was introduced for Chakma students. Prior to this, their education was in traditional Chakma script. A brief list of words has been made to locate genetic Chakma language, relative to their present and former neighbours and how closely they resemble to other groups of people.

	A list of Chakma words	*Meaning*
(1)	*Nakphul*	Nose Ornaments
(2)	*Kanphul, Jhomoli, Rajjure*	Ear Ornaments
(3)	*Bala Ban-guri, Banghu*	Wrist Ornaments
(4)	*Tajjur*	Arm Ornaments
(5)	*ThengatKhaur*	Ankle Ornaments
(6)	*Awjuli, Alchara*	Neck Ornaments
(7)	*BelUdana*	Sunrise
(8)	*Chung*	Child, dear
(9)	*Panee*	Water
(10)	*Panee-ban*	Flood
(11)	*Muro*	Hills
(12)	*Ngek (Nek)*	Husband
(13)	*Moogh*	Wife
(14)	*Beii*	Elder Sister
(15)	*Banai*	Brother-in-law
(16)	*Nanu*	Grandmother
(17)	*A-zoo*	Grand father
(18)	*Guzuri – Guzuri*	Lamenting
(19)	*Pade – Pade*	At all times
(20)	*Zadi – Zadi*	Quickly
(21)	*Lawge – Lawge*	Together
(22)	*Aa – dam*	Village

(Contd...)

(23)	*Chilum*	Dress
(24)	*Thum*	End
(25)	*Sing Kaba*	Sitting Room
(26)	*Pijor*	Front Machang
(27)	*Tem – Bang*	Discussion
(28)	*Paa – thru – thru*	Satisfaction, Content
(29)	*Zuu – Zuu*	Welcome
(30)	*Chebb*	Blessing by Elders
(31)	*Taba, Ujuna*	Cushine
(32)	*Teek – Kaba (Torbo)*	Shortcut Way
(33)	*Ranya*	After a jhumming is done on a spot of land, the Gap years for next jhumming is called – Ranya (barsen land)
(34)	*Aang*	Some words/numerals are used for protection from evils used in Arakan
(35)	*Bhadhya*	Food subscribed for ancestors (old Buddhist Custom)
(36)	*Rulli, Rouli*	Corrupt Buddhist monk in Arakan
(37)	*Magadha*	Wicked, deviousness
(38)	*Gozen*	Absolute truth (Gautama)
(39)	*Kyoung*	Monastery (origin Burmese word)

NB: A full paradism of Chakma nouns and verbs are needed to judge what similarities and differences are with respect of Indo-Aryan, Tibeto-Burman etc. languages.

Indo – Aryan	*Chakma*
(1) Jamai	Nek (Husband)
(2) Bou	Moog (Wife)
(3) Gali	Magadha (Wicked)
(4) Adar	Chitti / Chung (Dear)
(5) Namaskar	Zu-Zu (Welcome)
(6) Satya	Gozen (Truth)
(7) Picha	Pijor (Back part)
(8) Chalan	Sudam (Doctrine)
(9) Abhyas	Khaa-zek (Habit)

NB: The pronunciation of English "CH" becoming "TH" in Burmese like *Chak* become *Thak* : Chakma becomes Thakna (Tsakma), In Burmese, there is no "R" sound at all and that alphabets lack both "F" and "V". There are a very few aspirated consonants in the Chakma language. The alphabet 'K' in Bengali is like 'H' in chakma e.g. 'Khagendra' (Bengali) is 'Hagendra' (Chakma).

Assamese (Numericals)	**Chakma (Numericals)**
(1) EK	EK
(2) Dui	Dui
(3) Tini	Tin
(4) Sari	Sar
(5) Paas	Pas
(6) Sai	Sai
(7) Xaat	Xat
(8) Aati	Aat
(9) Na	Na

(Contd…)

(10)	Dah	Daws
(11)	Eghaara	Eghaara
(12)	Baara	Baara
(13)	Tera	Tera
(14)	Sauddha	Sauddha
(15)	Pandhara	Pandhara

NB: The ancient history of the Chakmas is not as transparent as that of the Ahom who ruled over Assam in the past. It is rather a far remote history. Many events have over taken them and they lean to trace their chronology from the Sakya race. L.A Waddel (1901 : 126) writes in the book, "The tribes of Brahmaputra valley", that the Chakma of CHT originally came from Assam and at that time they were known by nine Sub-Groups as below :-

1. Phawa – ho
2. Tai – ho
3. Ang – ngu
4. Bar – ua
5. Bung – ngu
6. Zolia
7. Beve – se – ke
8. Undu
9. Talia

It is known as "UNG" in Chal[illegible] [illegible]
symble of a MANTRA [illegible] [illegible]

Appendix

Hatch Way Serpents Tail Lions Smile

BE ON TO

Title's meaning:

Hatch–Way – A narrow passage connecting bountiful wealth, door in a spacecraft, devise a plot to etc.

Serpent's Tail – Commonly difficult to understand and unknown, it needs ability.

Lion's Smile – Generally thought to be unthinkable, but might be quite possible like

Enlightenment with profundity and depth.

The phrase above indicate – A person with status high or low (who can link with God) can be on to (Realise the significance or intentions of universal Buddhism)

Prologue

In a mysterious world phenomenon, two people play off against each other as opposition of equal shoulders for one's own end, purpose, without principle. That is how ever nations are threshed about wildly to dominate supremacy. There is no thoroughfare in this, the cosmos (world planet) is viewing Lion's smile or Serpent's tail to get smattering of such science of world affairs. This is interminable.

The rich nation's tapestry is known to be economic supremacy and the other is known to be spiritually advanced. This postulated confrontation of exploration of world's population and one cannot look upon them only for the time being, but it will result for change for future human existence in the earth, which is the fifth largest planet in the solar system, the earth is the only planet known to support life.

Human life is primarily on the basis of belief and chooses to believe in 'GOD', the supreme supernatural power (spirit). There are sacred things relating to spirit which is sometimes unknown and mystic relating to human birth and death. There are many scientific and philosophical studies. The children learn that their parents prayed to God, that is why God comes through him. What is the meaning of the word 'God'? That is inclination of human being with God, the spirit that has no death, like the cosmos which has no death (destruction). It can only transfigure on conditions. In Buddhism, it is "dependent origination" (Patitta Samudpada in Pali), and in meditative practice, it is the emptiness of transmission.

Why do the people decide on other's belief ? Why there is no positive belief in secularism (worldly, as opposed to sacred, not connected with religion)? There are extreme functions (act of anointing with oil in sacramental ceremony) in all the religions and other faith. All of them repeat prayers, a hatch way to inner wisdom of spectrum.

All supreme spiritual heads have their own way of explaining the great facts of human existence and also the cruel tyrannical problems. Dynamically world is changing at every moment and nothing is static as world is rotating ever and ever around the sun. It is beyond the human feeling, knowledge. The hatchway is the interest to take up time and give attention on Index 1 to 20.

Human sentient beings (having the power of perception by senses, feelings to mind) are the product of universe with greed, egotism at his command for life. Gautama Buddha had preached the highest stage of human development: there is no any enduring permanent self or substance, everything on process dependent origination. What is the ultimate reality of human life – when world is heading with modern ideas (thought) to replacing mind with highly mechanised elements like, computer (digital literacy) working with senses, like a community having a language is an important factor to create an illusion in their heart when it touches their senses (a magical spell)

Gautama Buddha preached his doctrine in Pali language, that was common for all (not restricted from spirituality only), and said "Sabbe satta Sukhita hantu (be all 'Satta' be happy. What is 'Satta'? In Buddhist philosophical term, all like Light and Darkness have compassion to be happy. It is dependent on one's understanding and knowledge, like material fibre optics can carry information in telephone, television and computer communication to the extent of great level.

Index

What is the percipient meaning of cosmos, Universe ?

In chemistry, precipitation make things to happen after filtration , throw, chemistry after filtration it to form, precipitating rain, snow etc. The cosmos (universe) is the whole of existing matter, energy, speed. The world is not a closed, harmonious, harmonic unity microcosmic (10-6) system; it is a battle ground of cross currents and inflicting contradictory purposes; it shows itself with pathetic obviousness as not a uni, but a multi verse (a material composition in general). It gives every sign of to be at variance and division within itself. It is ever and ever important to remember that whatever you create, you destroy and whatever you annihilate, you create – one condition the other, just as the inhalation conditions the exhalation (a puff or breath vapour), one is karmic result work of another i.e. relativism.

What is the planet EARTH ?

The fifth largest planet in the solar system, the earth, is the only planet known to support life. Between birth and death, the life circle. The earth has four main layers: a solid metal core with temperature of about 4,000 degree Celsius (7,200 degree Fahrenheit); a molten metal outer core; a mantle (shelf above a fire place), a metal composed largely of a rock called peridotite and the crust, of which there are two different types, continental and oceanic.

The earth is the centre of the Universe, all the stars, planets, galaxies in space, unoccupied area, inner and outer. Planet is a central body moving in an elliptical orbit round a star - a large body in space that revolves round the sun and the stars.

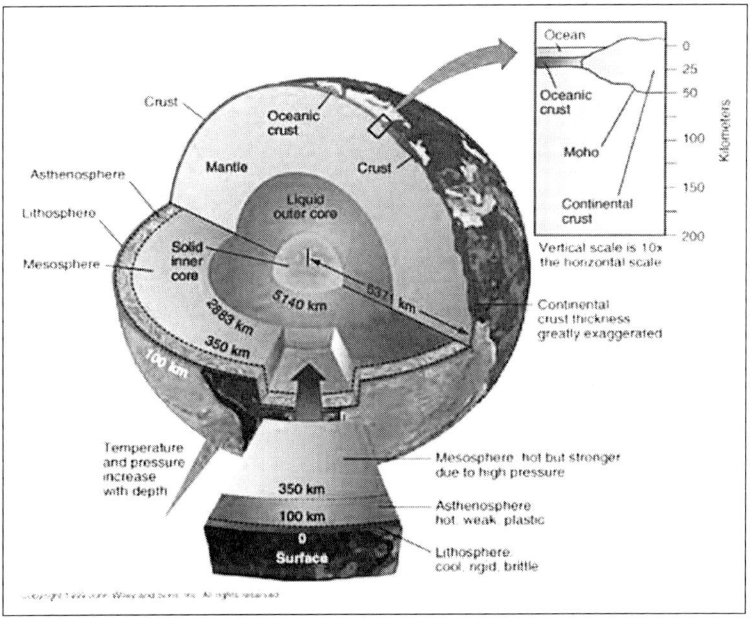

What is creation and human life ?

Creationism has the belief that the Universe and the living organisms originate from specific acts of divine creation. Human life is subjective experience into the field of perceived or imagined, where insight is possible. It is a complex unity, microcosmic (miniature representative of something), a thing that represents something much larger in physical form of understanding to. What is the meaning of mother? In Vedic religion, Kundalini is the mother of the universe and Shiva is the male power of the universe – an integrated whole of a living being. The understanding of life on the earth is an integrated whole of a living subjective imagined possible. It is like tears of manifestation of grief and happiness – their own cause of justifying. Look why human being has a lop-sided grain pattern, with one bigger, higher etc. than the other: not equally balanced, masterly mysterious.

How do you understand life on the Planet ?

Life on the planet manifests in two worlds, one is phenomenal (awareness about physical facts) and the other is spiritual world, which people cannot sense, like the rotation of world is not sensible to us. Look, how we are occupied and concerned with **Body → Eye → Nose → Ear → Tongue → Skin → Mind.** Look, how easy it is to confuse the pattern of religious diagram, shape as it is created along the cross current of beliefs of the world. Some say, before being adult, it is the joy of today and after being adult, it is the joy of mind and after that, the joy of patronage and home. There is a sacred thing relating to spirit which is something unknown and mystic. Those who take path in this track, they are spiritual persons.

What is SOUL ?

At the posterity of every religion (faith) there is a person's soul.

- Spiritual and immortal part of human being.
- Essential part of fundamental nature.
- Deep and sincere feelings.
- Person regarded as a typing some quality
- Person soulful (full of emotions)

The people accept the ideas, beliefs of their masters and those who preach spirituality are teachers of religion. There are a number of Gods and Goddesses representing a very soul. Vedic Hindu and many other faiths are stemming from the spirit and soul. Religion represents God and spirit which is egoistical oneself only, the sense of individual self. Any belief is just hiding your ignorance, knowing is transmission; knowledge is synthesis, integration of all is your potential. The vision of major religions groups like Vedic 5000 B.C. Christian 0 B.C. , Islam 7 A.D and Buddhism 560 B.C.

What is Vedic Religion ?

Rig-Veda, Sama-Veda, Ya-Jur-Veda, Atharva-Veda (latter collated into Upanishads) – all in Sanskrit, term around 1500 B.C. The most essential part of it is the true union link with "GOD" through 'I', soul or Yoga i.e. God + I (Hinduism). Children of 4 years learn - their parents prayed to God, that is why God come through him. "I link with GOD" i.e. "we are what we think" – systematic philosophies grew up gradually attempting to understand, realise and react against Vedic tenets from Gautama's time in 560 B.C .

In Hinduism, hierarchy is prevalent and hierarchically only a section of high priests by birth would make religious ceremonies. In Buddhism, these ceremonies are known to be

'Dhamma'. It is a crucial word in Buddhism. It has many forms and many interpretations. Gautama Buddha's the most doctrinal discourse is *Mahasatipatthana Sutta* mention that the four (4) methods of steadfast mindfulness are made up of fourteen (14) ways of contemplating the body, nine (9) ways of contemplating sensation, sixteen (16) ways of contemplating mind and five (5) ways of contemplating Dhamma (true reality).

What differs between senses and soul and Religion ?

David Hume (1711 – 1776 A.D) said, human has a mind and there is nothing in mind except what was first in the senses. The mind is at birth a clean sheet (a tabula rasa). Information and sense experience are written upon it in thousand ways: until sensation begets memory and memory begets ideas. The mind is not a substance or an organ that has ideas, it is only an abstract name of series of ideas. The perceptions: memorial and feelings are in mind. There is no observable 'soul' behind the process of thought.

The system of belief in worship of a supernatural power (spirit or God) has choreographed ceremonies in religion (Russian writer Leo Tolstoy in his book "How to get the hang of Buddhism"). Senses are organised to see, feel, hear, smell, touch when they are brought together with reality i.e. to see things as they are to perceive the truth.

What is Nature? Does the phenomenon of blood life relates to nature ?

The whole system of the existence, forces, and events of the physical world that are not controlled by human beings and the most essential qualities for existence is Nature.

All phenomena of the material world and person's outlook on life are interlinked. Undoubtedly, human beings are anthropocentric creature in this world and to become un-manifested from all that binds you is called liberation, in Vedic it is 'OM', 'Moksha' and in Buddhism, it is 'Nirvan'. The world's topmost divine masters have set up in their relationship to their followers a kind of culture, belief, tradition and religion in their point of view. In most advanced nations, they have set pace and some even no religion (secular). Human life, subjective imagined possible on will and emotions, a complex unity, micro cosmic (miniature representation of something), a thing that represents something much larger, indicating live, the nature of human consciousness, mental formation intentional, deliberate, aware, awake by five senses (hear, smell, taste, feel, desire) plus four elements air, water, soil, heat from senses mind consciousness beyond land, space, time (senses, mind, memory, idea). In science, consciousness describes matter and energy solely in terms of energy of space-time. Buddha describes matter, energy and material events as the structure of a fabric, we call consciousness.

The life of consciousness is a name of all practical thoughts and action justified by its fruits of consciousness. Reason is man's initiation of diversity. The life of reasons faced itself on science, because science contains all trustworthy knowledge. It is considered to be most powerful that religion can bring consciousness, egotistical virtue (excessively high opinion of oneself). Be mindful (conscious), aware (extra sensitive). Consciousness is systems of relationship of thoughts coincide illuminatingly with the sequences of events and relationship of things.

What was Gautama Buddha's ethnicity ?

As per the historian Herodotus, Gautama Buddha was born in Sakya race (Scythian in Central Asia). Also Ukrainians claim that Sakyas were precisely from the land that now belongs to Ukraine. European people originated about 6,000 years ago in the Ukraine. People left Ukraine and ended up all over the places or at the very least the culture and the language moved. According to modern research, Aryans were the first civilized people to settle in India proper and before that they came from Mesopotamia. The theory that Sanskrit speaking Aryans came from southern Russia has been controversial and is disputed.

However, while Buddha was an Aryan (noble) by upbringing, he was not an Aryan ethnically (Sakyan are from the scythians, Mongolian). Siddhartha was born around 563 B.C. in a rural province of Koshala kingdom located to the east of small river Achiravati on the road half away between Kapilavastu, the main town of the Sakyas (the family of the father) and Devadaha the main town of the Koliyas (family of the mother) This place is known as Lumbini in modern Nepal. Kosala was an Non-Aryan Kingdom.

The descendants of Sakya race and the followers of original Buddhist doctrines are a very small number and the beneficence of Buddha Dhamma can be seen outside India.

What is a Dream ?

It is a series of picture of events reflecting of a sleeping person, in distorted manner of past. Unconscious state of mind, sense while asleep, some cherished hope or thing in life. Dreams are private myth; myths are shared dreams.

What is Reflection?

Reflection of a surface or body throws back an image of, remind oneself. Sorrowful (unhappy) is not just to get rid of it. It is the reflective position that alludes to most important insight in Buddhism:

(a) There is Dukkha, just try to get rid of it;

(b) There may be endless Dukkha, stress;

(c) Accept, embrace it, develop mindfulness for understanding sepal of rumination.

What is Brain?

Brain is the co-ordinative centre of sensation and of intellectual and nervous activity. Brain sets in rumination stage. In sleep, the brain feeds and one become fresher after sleep: but the will, (determination, desire, mind, consists of understanding and will) requires no food. Hence, the need for sleep is greatest in brain workers, This fact however must not mislead us into extending sleep unduly: for then, it loses the intensity and become mere loss of time.

In sleep, the whole power in physical body, the inner strength of will is directed to the maintenance and improvement of organism.

What is Mind's Crevices?

AROUND THE WORLD

LION'S SHARE: A woman takes a selfie in front of an open-air cage of lions at the Tbilisi zoo that reopened on Sunday after it was destroyed by floods last June. Authorities in the Georgian capital had declared an emergency after tigers and wolves were set free in the streets after the floods

It is the element of a person that enables them to be aware of the world and their experiences to think and to feel: the faculty of consciousness and thought. One of the greatest thinkers of the world Gautama Buddha's preaching was of mind (chitta) : The man who is awake and strong can become fully purified, and becomes in the state of direct knowledge and power.

How does one understand DHAMMA Power ?

It is searing intensity of power for inner development (awakening). The term 'Dhamma' practice take the meaning with spirituality; toddling to rumination e.g. man's dependence on his environment, since world's environment are different from one area to another, people's physical and mental feature varies and so is 'Dhamma'. For human success and happiness, the most essential feature is to fit in well with the background – that is the Dhamma conviction, the soul of Buddhism. There is no priest by birth in Buddhism. Triple GEM (highly valued person or thing) is known to be 'Dhamma'. The term "Dhamma" is also used in religious term "Vipassana Dhamma". It is also integral part of our world view i.e. Dhamma dana, prayer and chanting. In Buddhism, the term Dhamma is the ultimate reality of all things (power): of all the real and final nature of matter (ontology) concerned with existence of mind and knowledge. The Universe is a mystery. Human mind cannot be absolutely destroyed with the human body and a strong belief prevails that there is some part of its which remains eternal – is it God, Divine or Dhamma !

What are four (4) types of sufferings in Buddhism ?

1. Birth is suffering for one in the natural period of life;
2. Sickness;
3. Aging;
4. Death.

These are natural things in Human Life.

Who is transmitter of life and what did they transmit to me?

There is a casual chain of 12 links of social character which is out of ignorance in the human world (dependent origination) in sharing common bond:

1. Ignorance (*avijja paccaya, sanskara*);
2. Karma potentialities, tendency inclined (natural) (*sanskara pratya vijana,* consciousness);
3. Embryonic in mother's womb (*vijnana pratya namarupa*);
4. Mind and body (*namarupa paccaya salayatana*);
5. Six (6) senses organs in Buddhism;
6. Senses object, contact memory;
7. Experience, sensation, vedana, undergo distilling fundamental difference of Buddhism and Hinduism in sensitivity to understand God, and in Buddhism Awareness I (illusion) is a link with god.
8. Craving, tanha, upadana;
9. Clinging upadana, Bhavana;
10. Re-Birth (becoming);
11. Decay, Jara (Suffering);
12. Death, Ending life

What is Advaya Buddhism and Hinduism ?

Do with purification, austerity, self-discipline, voluntarily self punishment to make amends of wrong doing, clear yourself as clear as day (certainly), clean up morally, cleanse clearly (well). Advaita Vedanta (Hindu) hints at conquest of all desires and sensual pleasure by practicing purity of thought, speech and action. In vedantic essential part of noble quality is the soul or Yoga (yuj=Yoke), true union of our god, unite or link with God through "I".

Gautama Buddha taught Dhamma to provide understanding of the void of true existence, concatenation (linked, joined) of events i.e. Paticca Samudpada in Pali and dependent origination in English through meditation "Anapana" and "Vipasana". The translation of Prajnaparamita Sutta (Pali) is Heart Sutta (English). The practice of real understanding is advaya – like the view of concept as animitta (no-form or non-determinate entity). *Advaya* means non-dual i.e. other than the two. The Skandhas are empty means as free from both being and non-being i.e. it mean Prajna – wisdom. Nagarjuna says – "We declare that whatever is interdependently originated is emptiness (shunyata). It is a conceptual designation of relativity of existence and is indeed the middle path". "No element can exist", he writes, "which does not participate interdependence, therefore no element which is not of the nature of emptiness can exist".

What does the term "Sankhya" means in Hindu and Buddhist Philosophy ?

In the philosophy, 'Sankaya' of upraised "OM", Moksha express the one un-manifested (freedom from all that binds you, freedom from all that is false, freedom from all that is going to die), the three manifest state of unconsciousness (body, speech and mind); whereas in Buddhism, it represents the meaning of body, speech and mind as duality, matter and mind. In a way (+ or -), the whole number is Zero or a thing complete itself. Buddhism is duality (matter and mind) and any theory denying the duality is known Monism, the doctrine that only Supreme Being exist (monistic), single, solipsistic.

Sankaya seeks a soul's liberation – the one God appears in many forms. He is in a thousand head, a thousand eye, a thousand feet like Vedic Vishnu rupa as well as Anekantaveda. The Jains believe in the soul and guided by the principle "Santhara" that is meant only for one who does not take food and resolved to part with the body to be united with the great soul – anthropocentric (it assumes that the whole creations are connected for men's purpose). "I" is link with God in all faith (religion) except Buddhism, where "I" is illusion and it must be realised through awareness, conscience. Whatever they do is divine by meditating at, it is just like breathing part of life.

What is saddest epoch incident in Gautama Buddha's life and what writ of visualisation was given by Buddha to Queen Vedehi ?

Gautama Buddha's biggest patron was Bhimbisara, the king of Rajgir, who was put to prison by his son and died of starvation. The queen Bedehi went to inform Buddha in a most disturbing and distressing way, while Buddha was in meditation. Having known the death of the king, Gautama Buddha in serene indifference of all the troubles around, gave visualisation (rumination) of pure-land in the space, where there is no pain. It is credulous to believe as said by a holy person – when Buddha said that 'Sarva Sanskara Anitya' (all sanskara are impermanent). She got the lighting effect of it on the spot.

CONCLUSION **(Hatchway Serpent's Tail Lion's Smile)**

In pali Dhammapada, verse no 183 (Hinayana scripture)

"Sabbapapassa Akaranam,

Kusalassa Upasampada,

Sacittapariyodapanam,

Etam Buddhana Sasanam"

In English, Mahayana Advaya Buddhism:

Do with purification, austerity, self-discipline, voluntary self, self-punishment

Clean yourself a clear day (certainly), cleans up (morally), cleanse clearly (well).

Unequivocally Expressing-

To avoid all evils;

To cultivate the good;

And to cleanse one's mind;

This is the teaching of Buddha.

This is essentially equal whether Hinayana, Theravada, Mahayana, Advaya, Pure land, lotus or western, Chinese, Japanese, Korean etc. in terms of Buddhism – Why ? In Buddhist Religious book Tripitaka (3 parts), all utterances of Gautama Buddha in "Sutra/Sutta" have been restored as it was committed to memory by his disciples. His first sermon to his first former companions (Buddha's first 4 noble truth) at Saranath forms the premise centre of Hinayana (Theravada) Buddhism. This earliest premise of Buddhism has not been rephrased. It is followed on the Buddha's earlier time by his followers (Theravadin) in India, Burma, Thailand, Cambodia, Sri-Lanka for individual Liberation (Arahat).

The other major schism of Buddhism is called Mahayana whose scripture is in Sanskrit and some in Pali. Their premise of belief in Gautama Buddha's prime discourse, the flower garden "Sutta" (Avatamsaka) for 21 days and other "Sutta" like pureland Buddhism (Gautama's preaching to queen Vedehi, Bimbisara's wife). The whole idea, understanding to like relativism, encompassed in it the idea of knowledge varies (it is not absolute or conditioned). Mahayana's basic background was laid by 1 AD by the leading philosopher Nagarjuna and founded Madhyamika in many contextual form of body to the layer whole universe. In Culasunnata Sutta, Buddha describes Sunnata – voidness of self, the fact on which it is established Dependent origination. Most of the Mahayana Sutras were delivered at Gridhrakuta mountain by Gautama Buddha.

So what actually Gautama had asked to do may be difficult to discern – but the central point is a worthy one: awake (Arahat, Gozen, Buddha). In essence, there are many fundamentally original Buddhist words like the term Gautama in Sanskrit and in Pali, GOZEN = ZEN (Dhammapada). Basically the origin of the term GOZEN/GOEII was from Saka =Sakya race community in Tibet and the Chakmas in CHT. Precisely, the top Buddhist learning centres in India were Vikramsila and Nalanda in Bihar and all scriptures were destroyed and Buddhists were massacred by Muslim invaders in 11-12 AD. In around 273 B.C, Ashoka became India's most powerful emperor when Buddhism was at the peak of existence. His patronage of Buddhism reached outside India like China, Burma (Myanmar), Sri Lanka and many other countries and transformation could be found in Buddhist way of salvation where it was perceived to continue through many re-births as Amitava Buddha (Bodhisattva) or enlightened beings. In later Mahayana School, the famous Chinese Buddhist monk Hiuen-Tsang stayed in Nalanda and carried the essence of Buddhism to China. Another famous Indian monk Atisa Dipankar Srijnan in 982 A.D carried Buddhism to Tibet and other countries. Some Buddhist ritual decorum are found in remote distant areas in India where ardent Buddhist took refuge, like the term "Siong", the food offering to a Buddhist monk who visits at the door for collection. Tibetan, Burmese, Arakanese and Chakmas have the common origin.

Dharma (Sanskrit) and Dhamma (Pali) are inimitable, the same in the nature of things, true reality (the eternal truth). It has been phrased and re-phrased like Dhamma – Chanting; Sanga; Prayer and others. In China and other countries, "Agama Sutra" (Buddha's preaching) relates with phenomenological object of direct experience. Both Dharma and Dhamma have choreographic ceremonies in religion of holy awareness.

Millennial Historical Events

Date / Time	Set of events
B.C 2500	(a) Members of Scythian tribes of central Asia ran over West Asia and South East Asia and Europe. (b) Members of Indus valley over-ran eastward invading Punjab. The Vedas, ancient sacred literature of Hindus were composed.
B.C 1000	(a) Scythians reached Yun-nan (now in china), Tibet (which is also in China) and Myanmar (Burma). (b) Members of Indus Valley reached beyond Punjab and composed Upanishads
B.C 600	(a) Scythians reached at the foot hills of the Himalayas. (b) The Indian sub-continent was ruled by 16 (sixteen great powers), besides smaller independent kingdoms. Sakyan (Saka) hailing from Scythians race was one of those tribal states.
B.C 560	(a) Birth of Gautama Buddha in Sakya clan for which he was known Saka/Sakyamuni. (b) The sphere of Sakya clan consolidated in the Himalayan ranges and valleys to Burma (Myanmar), Arakan Yoma and hill tracts of Chittagong (now in Bangladesh)
B.C 264	(a) Accession of the great emperor Ashoka whose patronage of Buddhism made way for propagation of Dhamma which Ashoka so internally felt, brought revolution of for bringing humanity and Gautama Buddha's Doctines to

	all over his kingdom and outside India (Sri Lanka, Burma) by sending his son and daughter as emissaries.
B.C 150	(a) The Stupas (dome) of Bharat and Sachi (b) The Buddhist philosopher Nagasena (c) The Milinda Panha (Questions of Milinda)
A.D 30	The rise of the Kusana dynesty and they extended their power in India. It played a major role in spreading light of Buddhism to far distant countries.
A.D 100	Progress of Mahayana school of Buddhism
A.D 125	Amaravati became an important Buddhist centre. It's worth noting the name Asvaghosa a leading Buddhist philosopher.
A.D 185	The Buddhist Philosopher Nagarjuna
A.D 375	The most splendid Ajanta Caves. The most recognised philosophers are Asanga, belonged to Hinayana set, lived in Ayodhya. Vasubandu, Santideva lived in Buddhist Monastery at Nalanda
A.D 630–644	The Chinese pilgrim Hiuen-Tsang visited India and studied Buddhism at Nalanda and there was another most leading Buddhist University Vikramsila, which has gone out of sight and untraceable
A.D 1100	The invader Muhammad Bakhtyar Khilji (a Turki) destroyed and massacred Buddhism in India. At that juncture, the invaders were overly proscriptive over Buddhist rituals and institutions. But by that time, Buddhist co-religious group already established worldwide and Buddhist population became nil except a select minority in North-East India.

An incontestable list of Arahat/Bodhisatva who had played a very important role in Buddhism is below:-

A.D. 1133 – 1212 Honor Japan
Pure Land

A.D. 1173 – 1262 Shinram Japan Pure Land

A.D. 1200 – 1253 Dogen Japan
Pure Land

A.D. 1546 – 1623 Han Shan China Pure Land

A.D. 1870 – 1966 Daisetsu – Suzuki Japan Zen

A.D. 1922 – 1996 Houn Jiyu Kennett Japan Zen

The task deciding whether a Buddhist monk has gained Arahatship or Bodhisattship does not fall on lay person. By standard procedure a Buddhist monk (in CHT) Sadhana Nanda Mahasthabir alias Bana Bhante (Bangladesh) augurs attainment of Arahatship from the experience of majority.

I think I will hang back a little while to give a major prominence of act of Sarvastivadin Buddhism in conducting Mangal Sutta (sutra) in a house hold. This ritual is performed when one recovers from illness, misfortune or in greetings for special occasion. As a ritual, an invitation is extended to a monk i.e. "fung" to be sent in advance, who will prepare the altar decorated with the offerings and plantain shoots and leaves round the whole room. The house mother's distaff (head rod on which wool etc. is wound for spinning) had been spun a long white thread, which circulates the altar and then carried into house, are held at the two end by the monk. After performing the ceremony, the layman devotees would tie up round the wrist from the distaff by the monks.

The central concept of Sakyan Theravada followers is sticking to Pali-Sruti. Indian languages have regional variation which was there even during Buddha's time. So he did not want to put his Dhamma in black and white. It was only after the

2nd world war, Buddhism reached America, Europe and the West with affiliated languages of the world with bigger patronisation, while the Sarvastivadin, the followers of ancient Buddhism are known for their cultural identity.

The ancient Sarvastivadin indigenous Buddhist population of the region suffered grave injustice over the last few decades. Mainstream dominant geo-politics starting with creation of independent nations of India and Pakistan nearly obliterated indigenous space and identity. A community was thus wronged by Colonial Great Britain as well as the new political establishments of India and Pakistan. The injustice to them continued though the dominant population of Bangladesh got liberation later. All political promises have turned to dust as their experiences. A good reflection can be taken from a writing of renowned intellectual Leo Tolstoy: "Friends, we shall never be; as you know yourself. But whatever we shall be the happiest people on earth or most wretched – that is in our hand". Theologically, the objective in Sarvastivada to achieve freedom from all sufferings, a high spiritual state is to be oneself alone.

Index

B

I

J

K

Index